Where I buried the bodies...
and other things you need to know when I'm gone

A Peace of Mind Planner & Organizer

BirdNerdPublishing.com
©Bird Nerd Publishing

The Importance of Planning

Our lives can be complicated, spread out, and confusing. So many things to keep track of and manage. When you passaway, will your loved ones easily be able to step in and sort through the details of your life?

This journal is designed to easily and effectively help you organize your life to make it easier for your loved ones to put your affairs in order after you pass; and because life changes, there's plenty of space for writing and lots of room to update information. This book is perfect for:
- Single People
- Couples & Families
- Business Owners
- Property Owners

A few suggestions when organizing your information:
- Much of the information for this journal can be entered in a few different places so put it in the location that makes the most sense for you. For example, in the *Financial Section* you can enter username and passwords for online banking, however you might choose to enter all user names and passwords in the master *Password Section*.
- You might consider assembling a box or binder with all your important documents (birth certificates, social security cards, etc) in one central location.
- **Keep this journal in a very safe place**... your entire life is in it. Plus, do you really want those bodies discovered while you're still around?

My hope for this journal is that it brings you peace of mind knowing that you've gone above and beyond to make sure your family is taken care of.

Table of Contents

About Me

NAME		
STREET ADDRESS		
CITY	STATE	ZIP
HOME PHONE		
CELL PHONE		
EMAIL ADDRESS		
SOCIAL SECURITY #		
DRIVERS LICENSE #		
PASSPORT #		
DATE OF BIRTH	LOCATION	
FATHER'S NAME		
MOTHER'S NAME		

EMPLOYER		
STREET ADDRESS		
CITY	STATE	ZIP
PHONE		
EMAIL		

PRIMARY CARE PHYSICIAN		
STREET ADDRESS		
CITY	STATE	ZIP
PHONE		

INSURANCE		
GROUP #		
POLICY #		
PHONE		

INSURANCE		
GROUP #		
POLICY #		
PHONE		

My Partner

NAME		
STREET ADDRESS		
CITY	STATE	ZIP
HOME PHONE		
CELL PHONE		
EMAIL ADDRESS		
SOCIAL SECURITY #		
DRIVERS LICENSE #		
PASSPORT #		
DATE OF BIRTH	LOCATION	
FATHER'S NAME		
MOTHER'S NAME		

EMPLOYER		
STREET ADDRESS		
CITY	STATE	ZIP
PHONE		
EMAIL		

PRIMARY CARE PHYSICIAN		
STREET ADDRESS		
CITY	STATE	ZIP
PHONE		

INSURANCE
GROUP #
POLICY #
PHONE

INSURANCE
GROUP #
POLICY #
PHONE

Children

NAME		
STREET ADDRESS		
CITY	STATE	ZIP
CELL PHONE		
SOCIAL SECURITY #		
DATE OF BIRTH	LOCATION	
FATHER'S NAME		
MOTHER'S NAME		

SCHOOL		
STREET ADDRESS		
CITY	STATE	ZIP
PHONE		

EMPLOYER		
STREET ADDRESS		
CITY	STATE	ZIP
PHONE		

PRIMARY CARE PHYSICIAN		
STREET ADDRESS		
CITY	STATE	ZIP
PHONE		

DENTIST		
STREET ADDRESS		
CITY	STATE	ZIP
PHONE		

INSURANCE		
GROUP #		
POLICY #		
PHONE		

Children

NAME			
STREET ADDRESS			
CITY	STATE	ZIP	
CELL PHONE			
SOCIAL SECURITY #			
DATE OF BIRTH	LOCATION		
FATHER'S NAME			
MOTHER'S NAME			

SCHOOL		
STREET ADDRESS		
CITY	STATE	ZIP
PHONE		

EMPLOYER		
STREET ADDRESS		
CITY	STATE	ZIP
PHONE		

PRIMARY CARE PHYSICIAN		
STREET ADDRESS		
CITY	STATE	ZIP
PHONE		

DENTIST		
STREET ADDRESS		
CITY	STATE	ZIP
PHONE		

INSURANCE
GROUP #
POLICY #
PHONE

Children

NAME			
STREET ADDRESS			
CITY	STATE	ZIP	
CELL PHONE			
SOCIAL SECURITY #			
DATE OF BIRTH	LOCATION		
FATHER'S NAME			
MOTHER'S NAME			

SCHOOL		
STREET ADDRESS		
CITY	STATE	ZIP
PHONE		

EMPLOYER		
STREET ADDRESS		
CITY	STATE	ZIP
PHONE		

PRIMARY CARE PHYSICIAN		
STREET ADDRESS		
CITY	STATE	ZIP
PHONE		

DENTIST		
STREET ADDRESS		
CITY	STATE	ZIP
PHONE		

INSURANCE
GROUP #
POLICY #
PHONE

Children

NAME		
STREET ADDRESS		
CITY	STATE	ZIP
CELL PHONE		
SOCIAL SECURITY #		
DATE OF BIRTH	LOCATION	
FATHER'S NAME		
MOTHER'S NAME		

SCHOOL		
STREET ADDRESS		
CITY	STATE	ZIP
PHONE		

EMPLOYER		
STREET ADDRESS		
CITY	STATE	ZIP
PHONE		

PRIMARY CARE PHYSICIAN		
STREET ADDRESS		
CITY	STATE	ZIP
PHONE		

DENTIST		
STREET ADDRESS		
CITY	STATE	ZIP
PHONE		

INSURANCE
GROUP #
POLICY #
PHONE

Children

NAME	
STREET ADDRESS	
CITY	STATE ZIP
CELL PHONE	
SOCIAL SECURITY #	
DATE OF BIRTH	LOCATION
FATHER'S NAME	
MOTHER'S NAME	

SCHOOL	
STREET ADDRESS	
CITY	STATE ZIP
PHONE	

EMPLOYER	
STREET ADDRESS	
CITY	STATE ZIP
PHONE	

PRIMARY CARE PHYSICIAN	
STREET ADDRESS	
CITY	STATE ZIP
PHONE	

DENTIST	
STREET ADDRESS	
CITY	STATE ZIP
PHONE	

INSURANCE	
GROUP #	
POLICY #	
PHONE	

That Sibling I Forgot to Mention

NAME	
STREET ADDRESS	
CITY	STATE ZIP
CELL PHONE	
SOCIAL SECURITY #	
DATE OF BIRTH	LOCATION
FATHER'S NAME	
MOTHER'S NAME	

SCHOOL	
STREET ADDRESS	
CITY	STATE ZIP
PHONE	

EMPLOYER	
STREET ADDRESS	
CITY	STATE ZIP
PHONE	

PRIMARY CARE PHYSICIAN	
STREET ADDRESS	
CITY	STATE ZIP
PHONE	

DENTIST	
STREET ADDRESS	
CITY	STATE ZIP
PHONE	

INSURANCE	
GROUP #	
POLICY #	
PHONE	

Pets

NAME	
BREED / DESCRIPTION	
MICROCHIP #	
VETERINARIAN	
STREET ADDRESS	
CITY	STATE ZIP
MEDICATIONS	
NOTES	

NAME	
BREED / DESCRIPTION	
MICROCHIP #	
VETERINARIAN	
STREET ADDRESS	
CITY	STATE ZIP
MEDICATIONS	
NOTES	

NAME	
BREED / DESCRIPTION	
MICROCHIP #	
VETERINARIAN	
STREET ADDRESS	
CITY	STATE ZIP
MEDICATIONS	
NOTES	

Pets

NAME

BREED / DESCRIPTION

MICROCHIP #

VETERINARIAN

STREET ADDRESS

CITY   STATE   ZIP

MEDICATIONS

NOTES

NAME

BREED / DESCRIPTION

MICROCHIP #

VETERINARIAN

STREET ADDRESS

CITY   STATE   ZIP

MEDICATIONS

NOTES

NAME

BREED / DESCRIPTION

MICROCHIP #

VETERINARIAN

STREET ADDRESS

CITY   STATE   ZIP

MEDICATIONS

NOTES

Pets

NAME			
BREED / DESCRIPTION			
MICROCHIP #			
VETERINARIAN			
STREET ADDRESS			
CITY	STATE	ZIP	
MEDICATIONS			
NOTES			

NAME			
BREED / DESCRIPTION			
MICROCHIP #			
VETERINARIAN			
STREET ADDRESS			
CITY	STATE	ZIP	
MEDICATIONS			
NOTES			

NAME			
BREED / DESCRIPTION			
MICROCHIP #			
VETERINARIAN			
STREET ADDRESS			
CITY	STATE	ZIP	
MEDICATIONS			
NOTES			

Pets

NAME	
BREED / DESCRIPTION	
MICROCHIP #	
VETERINARIAN	
STREET ADDRESS	
CITY	STATE ZIP
MEDICATIONS	
NOTES	

NAME	
BREED / DESCRIPTION	
MICROCHIP #	
VETERINARIAN	
STREET ADDRESS	
CITY	STATE ZIP
MEDICATIONS	
NOTES	

NAME	
BREED / DESCRIPTION	
MICROCHIP #	
VETERINARIAN	
STREET ADDRESS	
CITY	STATE ZIP
MEDICATIONS	
NOTES	

Home Details

STREET ADDRESS			
CITY		STATE	ZIP

ACCESS INFORMATION

HOUSE CODE
GARAGE CODE
KEY LOCATION

WiFI / NETWORK

WiFi NETWORK NAME	
WiFi PASSWORD	
SERVER PASSWORD	
ROUTER LOCATION	
INTERNET PROVIDER	
ACCOUNT NUMBER	
USERNAME	
PASSWORD	❏ SEE PASSWORDS

SCHEDULES

TRASH PICKUP
LAWN CARE
CLEANING

MORTGAGE / LANDLORD INFORMATION

BANK		
CONTACT		
PHONE		
STREET ADDRESS		
CITY	STATE	ZIP
ACCOUNT #		
WEBSITE		
USERNAME		
PASSWORD		❏ SEE PASSWORDS

Home Details

STREET ADDRESS		
CITY	STATE	ZIP

ACCESS INFORMATION

HOUSE CODE
GARAGE CODE
KEY LOCATION

WiFI / NETWORK

WiFi NETWORK NAME
WiFi PASSWORD
SERVER PASSWORD
ROUTER LOCATION
INTERNET PROVIDER
ACCOUNT NUMBER
USERNAME
PASSWORD   ❏ SEE PASSWORDS

SCHEDULES

TRASH PICKUP
LAWN CARE
CLEANING

MORTGAGE / LANDLORD INFORMATION

BANK		
CONTACT		
PHONE		
STREET ADDRESS		
CITY	STATE	ZIP
ACCOUNT #		
WEBSITE		
USERNAME		
PASSWORD		❏ SEE PASSWORDS

Business / Real Estate

TENANT		
BUSINESS NAME		
STREET ADDRESS		
CITY	STATE	ZIP
MONTHLY RENT	DUE	

ACCESS INFORMATION

HOUSE / BUILDING CODE
GARAGE CODE
KEY LOCATION

WiFI / NETWORK

WiFi NETWORK NAME
WiFi PASSWORD
SERVER PASSWORD
ROUTER LOCATION

SCHEDULES

TRASH PICKUP
LAWN CARE
CLEANING

MORTGAGE / LANDLORD INFORMATION

LANDLORD		
BANK		
CONTACT		
PHONE		
STREET ADDRESS		
CITY	STATE	ZIP
ACCOUNT #		
WEBSITE		
USERNAME		
PASSWORD		❑ SEE PASSWORDS

Business / Real Estate

TENANT		
BUSINESS NAME		
STREET ADDRESS		
CITY	STATE	ZIP
MONTHLY RENT	DUE	

ACCESS INFORMATION

HOUSE / BUILDING CODE
GARAGE CODE
KEY LOCATION

WiFI / NETWORK

WiFi NETWORK NAME
WiFi PASSWORD
SERVER PASSWORD
ROUTER LOCATION

SCHEDULES

TRASH PICKUP
LAWN CARE
CLEANING

MORTGAGE / LANDLORD INFORMATION

LANDLORD		
BANK		
CONTACT		
PHONE		
STREET ADDRESS		
CITY	STATE	ZIP
ACCOUNT #		
WEBSITE		
USERNAME		
PASSWORD		❑ SEE PASSWORDS

Business / Real Estate

TENANT			
BUSINESS NAME			
STREET ADDRESS			
CITY	STATE	ZIP	
MONTHLY RENT	DUE		

ACCESS INFORMATION

HOUSE / BUILDING CODE
GARAGE CODE
KEY LOCATION

WiFI / NETWORK

WiFi NETWORK NAME
WiFi PASSWORD
SERVER PASSWORD
ROUTER LOCATION

SCHEDULES

TRASH PICKUP
LAWN CARE
CLEANING

MORTGAGE / LANDLORD INFORMATION

LANDLORD			
BANK			
CONTACT			
PHONE			
STREET ADDRESS			
CITY	STATE	ZIP	
ACCOUNT #			
WEBSITE			
USERNAME			
PASSWORD			❑ SEE PASSWORDS

Business / Real Estate

TENANT	
BUSINESS NAME	
STREET ADDRESS	
CITY	*STATE* *ZIP*
MONTHLY RENT	*DUE*

ACCESS INFORMATION
HOUSE / BUILDING CODE
GARAGE CODE
KEY LOCATION

WiFI / NETWORK
WiFi NETWORK NAME
WiFi PASSWORD
SERVER PASSWORD
ROUTER LOCATION

SCHEDULES
TRASH PICKUP
LAWN CARE
CLEANING

MORTGAGE / LANDLORD INFORMATION	
LANDLORD	
BANK	
CONTACT	
PHONE	
STREET ADDRESS	
CITY	*STATE* *ZIP*
ACCOUNT #	
WEBSITE	
USERNAME	
PASSWORD	❑ *SEE PASSWORDS*

Business / Real Estate

TENANT			
BUSINESS NAME			
STREET ADDRESS			
CITY		STATE	ZIP
MONTHLY RENT		DUE	

ACCESS INFORMATION

HOUSE / BUILDING CODE
GARAGE CODE
KEY LOCATION

WiFI / NETWORK

WiFi NETWORK NAME
WiFi PASSWORD
SERVER PASSWORD
ROUTER LOCATION

SCHEDULES

TRASH PICKUP
LAWN CARE
CLEANING

MORTGAGE / LANDLORD INFORMATION

LANDLORD			
BANK			
CONTACT			
PHONE			
STREET ADDRESS			
CITY		STATE	ZIP
ACCOUNT #			
WEBSITE			
USERNAME			
PASSWORD			❏ SEE PASSWORDS

Business / Real Estate

TENANT	
BUSINESS NAME	
STREET ADDRESS	
CITY	*STATE*　　　*ZIP*
MONTHLY RENT	*DUE*

ACCESS INFORMATION

HOUSE / BUILDING CODE
GARAGE CODE
KEY LOCATION

WiFI / NETWORK

WiFi NETWORK NAME
WiFi PASSWORD
SERVER PASSWORD
ROUTER LOCATION

SCHEDULES

TRASH PICKUP
LAWN CARE
CLEANING

MORTGAGE / LANDLORD INFORMATION

LANDLORD	
BANK	
CONTACT	
PHONE	
STREET ADDRESS	
CITY	*STATE*　　　*ZIP*
ACCOUNT #	
WEBSITE	
USERNAME	
PASSWORD	❏ *SEE PASSWORDS*

Business / Real Estate

TENANT		
BUSINESS NAME		
STREET ADDRESS		
CITY	STATE	ZIP
MONTHLY RENT	DUE	

ACCESS INFORMATION

HOUSE / BUILDING CODE
GARAGE CODE
KEY LOCATION

WiFI / NETWORK

WiFi NETWORK NAME
WiFi PASSWORD
SERVER PASSWORD
ROUTER LOCATION

SCHEDULES

TRASH PICKUP
LAWN CARE
CLEANING

MORTGAGE / LANDLORD INFORMATION

LANDLORD		
BANK		
CONTACT		
PHONE		
STREET ADDRESS		
CITY	STATE	ZIP
ACCOUNT #		
WEBSITE		
USERNAME		
PASSWORD		❑ SEE PASSWORDS

The Vacation Home I
Never Told You About

TENANT		
BUSINESS NAME		
STREET ADDRESS		
CITY	*STATE*	*ZIP*
MONTHLY RENT	*DUE*	

ACCESS INFORMATION

HOUSE / BUILDING CODE
GARAGE CODE
KEY LOCATION

WiFI / NETWORK

WiFi NETWORK NAME
WiFi PASSWORD
SERVER PASSWORD
ROUTER LOCATION

SCHEDULES

TRASH PICKUP
LAWN CARE
CLEANING

MORTGAGE / LANDLORD INFORMATION

LANDLORD		
BANK		
CONTACT		
PHONE		
STREET ADDRESS		
CITY	*STATE*	*ZIP*
ACCOUNT #		
WEBSITE		
USERNAME		
PASSWORD		❑ *SEE PASSWORDS*

Vehicles

MAKE	
MODEL	
LICENSE NUMBER	
VEHICLE LOCATION	
KEY LOCATION	
INSURANCE COMPANY	
POLICY NUMBER	
WEBSITE	
USERNAME	
PASSWORD	❑ SEE PASSWORDS
LOAN COMPANY	
ACCOUNT #	
WEBSITE	
USERNAME	
PASSWORD	❑ SEE PASSWORDS

MAKE	
MODEL	
LICENSE NUMBER	
VEHICLE LOCATION	
KEY LOCATION	
INSURANCE COMPANY	
POLICY NUMBER	
WEBSITE	
USERNAME	
PASSWORD	❑ SEE PASSWORDS
LOAN COMPANY	
ACCOUNT #	
WEBSITE	
USERNAME	
PASSWORD	❑ SEE PASSWORDS

Vehicles

MAKE

MODEL

LICENSE NUMBER

VEHICLE LOCATION

KEY LOCATION

INSURANCE COMPANY

POLICY NUMBER

WEBSITE

USERNAME

PASSWORD   ❏ SEE PASSWORDS

LOAN COMPANY

ACCOUNT #

WEBSITE

USERNAME

PASSWORD   ❏ SEE PASSWORDS

MAKE

MODEL

LICENSE NUMBER

VEHICLE LOCATION

KEY LOCATION

INSURANCE COMPANY

POLICY NUMBER

WEBSITE

USERNAME

PASSWORD   ❏ SEE PASSWORDS

LOAN COMPANY

ACCOUNT #

WEBSITE

USERNAME

PASSWORD   ❏ SEE PASSWORDS

Vehicles

MAKE	
MODEL	
LICENSE NUMBER	
VEHICLE LOCATION	
KEY LOCATION	
INSURANCE COMPANY	
POLICY NUMBER	
WEBSITE	
USERNAME	
PASSWORD	❏ SEE PASSWORDS
LOAN COMPANY	
ACCOUNT #	
WEBSITE	
USERNAME	
PASSWORD	❏ SEE PASSWORDS

MAKE	
MODEL	
LICENSE NUMBER	
VEHICLE LOCATION	
KEY LOCATION	
INSURANCE COMPANY	
POLICY NUMBER	
WEBSITE	
USERNAME	
PASSWORD	❏ SEE PASSWORDS
LOAN COMPANY	
ACCOUNT #	
WEBSITE	
USERNAME	
PASSWORD	❏ SEE PASSWORDS

Vehicles

MAKE	
MODEL	
LICENSE NUMBER	
VEHICLE LOCATION	
KEY LOCATION	
INSURANCE COMPANY	
POLICY NUMBER	
WEBSITE	
USERNAME	
PASSWORD	❏ SEE PASSWORDS
LOAN COMPANY	
ACCOUNT #	
WEBSITE	
USERNAME	
PASSWORD	❏ SEE PASSWORDS

MAKE	
MODEL	
LICENSE NUMBER	
VEHICLE LOCATION	
KEY LOCATION	
INSURANCE COMPANY	
POLICY NUMBER	
WEBSITE	
USERNAME	
PASSWORD	❏ SEE PASSWORDS
LOAN COMPANY	
ACCOUNT #	
WEBSITE	
USERNAME	
PASSWORD	❏ SEE PASSWORDS

Vehicles

MAKE	
MODEL	
LICENSE NUMBER	
VEHICLE LOCATION	
KEY LOCATION	
INSURANCE COMPANY	
POLICY NUMBER	
WEBSITE	
USERNAME	
PASSWORD	❏ SEE PASSWORDS
LOAN COMPANY	
ACCOUNT #	
WEBSITE	
USERNAME	
PASSWORD	❏ SEE PASSWORDS

MAKE	
MODEL	
LICENSE NUMBER	
VEHICLE LOCATION	
KEY LOCATION	
INSURANCE COMPANY	
POLICY NUMBER	
WEBSITE	
USERNAME	
PASSWORD	❏ SEE PASSWORDS
LOAN COMPANY	
ACCOUNT #	
WEBSITE	
USERNAME	
PASSWORD	❏ SEE PASSWORDS

Vehicles

MAKE	
MODEL	
LICENSE NUMBER	
VEHICLE LOCATION	
KEY LOCATION	
INSURANCE COMPANY	
POLICY NUMBER	
WEBSITE	
USERNAME	
PASSWORD	❏ SEE PASSWORDS
LOAN COMPANY	
ACCOUNT #	
WEBSITE	
USERNAME	
PASSWORD	❏ SEE PASSWORDS

MAKE	
MODEL	
LICENSE NUMBER	
VEHICLE LOCATION	
KEY LOCATION	
INSURANCE COMPANY	
POLICY NUMBER	
WEBSITE	
USERNAME	
PASSWORD	❏ SEE PASSWORDS
LOAN COMPANY	
ACCOUNT #	
WEBSITE	
USERNAME	
PASSWORD	❏ SEE PASSWORDS

Vehicles

MAKE	
MODEL	
LICENSE NUMBER	
VEHICLE LOCATION	
KEY LOCATION	
INSURANCE COMPANY	
POLICY NUMBER	
WEBSITE	
USERNAME	
PASSWORD	❏ SEE PASSWORDS
LOAN COMPANY	
ACCOUNT #	
WEBSITE	
USERNAME	
PASSWORD	❏ SEE PASSWORDS

MAKE	
MODEL	
LICENSE NUMBER	
VEHICLE LOCATION	
KEY LOCATION	
INSURANCE COMPANY	
POLICY NUMBER	
WEBSITE	
USERNAME	
PASSWORD	❏ SEE PASSWORDS
LOAN COMPANY	
ACCOUNT #	
WEBSITE	
USERNAME	
PASSWORD	❏ SEE PASSWORDS

Vehicles

MAKE	
MODEL	
LICENSE NUMBER	
VEHICLE LOCATION	
KEY LOCATION	
INSURANCE COMPANY	
POLICY NUMBER	
WEBSITE	
USERNAME	
PASSWORD	❏ SEE PASSWORDS
LOAN COMPANY	
ACCOUNT #	
WEBSITE	
USERNAME	
PASSWORD	❏ SEE PASSWORDS

MAKE	
MODEL	
LICENSE NUMBER	
VEHICLE LOCATION	
KEY LOCATION	
INSURANCE COMPANY	
POLICY NUMBER	
WEBSITE	
USERNAME	
PASSWORD	❏ SEE PASSWORDS
LOAN COMPANY	
ACCOUNT #	
WEBSITE	
USERNAME	
PASSWORD	❏ SEE PASSWORDS

Security / Storage

SAFETY DEPOSIT BOX		
BANK		
STREET ADDRESS		
CITY	STATE	ZIP
BOX NUMBER	KEY LOCATION	
CONTENTS:		

SAFE		
LOCATION		
STREET ADDRESS		
CITY	STATE	ZIP
COMBINATION	KEY LOCATION	
CONTENTS:		

STORAGE UNIT		
LOCATION		
STREET ADDRESS		
CITY	STATE	ZIP
COMBINATION	KEY LOCATION	
CONTENTS:		

STORAGE UNIT		
LOCATION		
STREET ADDRESS		
CITY	STATE	ZIP
COMBINATION	KEY LOCATION	
CONTENTS:		

Security

SECURITY SYSTEM - HOME		
ARM CODE		
DISARM CODE		
MONITORING COMPANY		
STREET ADDRESS		
CITY	STATE	ZIP
ACCOUNT NUMBER		
WEBSITE		
USERNAME		
PASSWORD		❏ SEE PASSWORDS

SECURITY SYSTEM - BUSINESS		
ARM CODE		
DISARM CODE		
MONITORING COMPANY		
STREET ADDRESS		
CITY	STATE	ZIP
ACCOUNT NUMBER		
WEBSITE		
USERNAME		
PASSWORD		❏ SEE PASSWORDS

SECURITY SYSTEM - OTHER		
ARM CODE		
DISARM CODE		
MONITORING COMPANY		
STREET ADDRESS		
CITY	STATE	ZIP
ACCOUNT NUMBER		
WEBSITE		
USERNAME		
PASSWORD		❏ SEE PASSWORDS

Device Passwords

❏ *PHONE*   ❏ *COMPUTER*   ❏ *TABLET*   ❏ *OTHER*

USERNAME

PASSWORD/PASSCODE

❏ *PHONE*   ❏ *COMPUTER*   ❏ *TABLET*   ❏ *OTHER*

USERNAME

PASSWORD/PASSCODE

❏ *PHONE*   ❏ *COMPUTER*   ❏ *TABLET*   ❏ *OTHER*

USERNAME

PASSWORD/PASSCODE

❏ *PHONE*   ❏ *COMPUTER*   ❏ *TABLET*   ❏ *OTHER*

USERNAME

PASSWORD/PASSCODE

❏ *PHONE*   ❏ *COMPUTER*   ❏ *TABLET*   ❏ *OTHER*

USERNAME

PASSWORD/PASSCODE

❏ *PHONE*   ❏ *COMPUTER*   ❏ *TABLET*   ❏ *OTHER*

USERNAME

PASSWORD/PASSCODE

❏ *PHONE*   ❏ *COMPUTER*   ❏ *TABLET*   ❏ *OTHER*

USERNAME

PASSWORD/PASSCODE

❏ *PHONE*   ❏ *COMPUTER*   ❏ *TABLET*   ❏ *OTHER*

USERNAME

PASSWORD/PASSCODE

❏ *PHONE*   ❏ *COMPUTER*   ❏ *TABLET*   ❏ *OTHER*

USERNAME

PASSWORD/PASSCODE

Device Passwords

❑ *PHONE*   ❑ *COMPUTER*   ❑ *TABLET*   ❑ *OTHER*

USERNAME

PASSWORD/PASSCODE

❑ *PHONE*   ❑ *COMPUTER*   ❑ *TABLET*   ❑ *OTHER*

USERNAME

PASSWORD/PASSCODE

❑ *PHONE*   ❑ *COMPUTER*   ❑ *TABLET*   ❑ *OTHER*

USERNAME

PASSWORD/PASSCODE

❑ *PHONE*   ❑ *COMPUTER*   ❑ *TABLET*   ❑ *OTHER*

USERNAME

PASSWORD/PASSCODE

❑ *PHONE*   ❑ *COMPUTER*   ❑ *TABLET*   ❑ *OTHER*

USERNAME

PASSWORD/PASSCODE

❑ *PHONE*   ❑ *COMPUTER*   ❑ *TABLET*   ❑ *OTHER*

USERNAME

PASSWORD/PASSCODE

❑ *PHONE*   ❑ *COMPUTER*   ❑ *TABLET*   ❑ *OTHER*

USERNAME

PASSWORD/PASSCODE

❑ *PHONE*   ❑ *COMPUTER*   ❑ *TABLET*   ❑ *OTHER*

USERNAME

PASSWORD/PASSCODE

❑ *PHONE*   ❑ *COMPUTER*   ❑ *TABLET*   ❑ *OTHER*

USERNAME

PASSWORD/PASSCODE

Device Passwords

❑ *PHONE*   ❑ *COMPUTER*   ❑ *TABLET*   ❑ *OTHER*

USERNAME

PASSWORD/PASSCODE

❑ *PHONE*   ❑ *COMPUTER*   ❑ *TABLET*   ❑ *OTHER*

USERNAME

PASSWORD/PASSCODE

❑ *PHONE*   ❑ *COMPUTER*   ❑ *TABLET*   ❑ *OTHER*

USERNAME

PASSWORD/PASSCODE

❑ *PHONE*   ❑ *COMPUTER*   ❑ *TABLET*   ❑ *OTHER*

USERNAME

PASSWORD/PASSCODE

❑ *PHONE*   ❑ *COMPUTER*   ❑ *TABLET*   ❑ *OTHER*

USERNAME

PASSWORD/PASSCODE

❑ *PHONE*   ❑ *COMPUTER*   ❑ *TABLET*   ❑ *OTHER*

USERNAME

PASSWORD/PASSCODE

❑ *PHONE*   ❑ *COMPUTER*   ❑ *TABLET*   ❑ *OTHER*

USERNAME

PASSWORD/PASSCODE

❑ *PHONE*   ❑ *COMPUTER*   ❑ *TABLET*   ❑ *OTHER*

USERNAME

PASSWORD/PASSCODE

❑ *PHONE*   ❑ *COMPUTER*   ❑ *TABLET*   ❑ *OTHER*

USERNAME

PASSWORD/PASSCODE

Device Passwords

❏ PHONE ❏ COMPUTER ❏ TABLET ❏ OTHER
USERNAME
PASSWORD/PASSCODE

❏ PHONE ❏ COMPUTER ❏ TABLET ❏ OTHER
USERNAME
PASSWORD/PASSCODE

❏ PHONE ❏ COMPUTER ❏ TABLET ❏ OTHER
USERNAME
PASSWORD/PASSCODE

❏ PHONE ❏ COMPUTER ❏ TABLET ❏ OTHER
USERNAME
PASSWORD/PASSCODE

❏ PHONE ❏ COMPUTER ❏ TABLET ❏ OTHER
USERNAME
PASSWORD/PASSCODE

❏ PHONE ❏ COMPUTER ❏ TABLET ❏ OTHER
USERNAME
PASSWORD/PASSCODE

❏ PHONE ❏ COMPUTER ❏ TABLET ❏ OTHER
USERNAME
PASSWORD/PASSCODE

❏ PHONE ❏ COMPUTER ❏ TABLET ❏ OTHER
USERNAME
PASSWORD/PASSCODE

❏ PHONE ❏ COMPUTER ❏ TABLET ❏ OTHER
USERNAME
PASSWORD/PASSCODE

Online Passwords

WEBSITE	
PURPOSE	
USERNAME	
PASSWORD	
SECURITY QUESTION	
ANSWER	
SECURITY QUESTION	
ANSWER	
SECURITY QUESTION	
ANSWER	

WEBSITE	
PURPOSE	
USERNAME	
PASSWORD	
SECURITY QUESTION	
ANSWER	
SECURITY QUESTION	
ANSWER	
SECURITY QUESTION	
ANSWER	

WEBSITE	
PURPOSE	
USERNAME	
PASSWORD	
SECURITY QUESTION	
ANSWER	
SECURITY QUESTION	
ANSWER	
SECURITY QUESTION	
ANSWER	

Online Passwords

WEBSITE	
PURPOSE	
USERNAME	
PASSWORD	
SECURITY QUESTION	
ANSWER	
SECURITY QUESTION	
ANSWER	
SECURITY QUESTION	
ANSWER	

WEBSITE	
PURPOSE	
USERNAME	
PASSWORD	
SECURITY QUESTION	
ANSWER	
SECURITY QUESTION	
ANSWER	
SECURITY QUESTION	
ANSWER	

WEBSITE	
PURPOSE	
USERNAME	
PASSWORD	
SECURITY QUESTION	
ANSWER	
SECURITY QUESTION	
ANSWER	
SECURITY QUESTION	
ANSWER	

Online Passwords

WEBSITE	
PURPOSE	
USERNAME	
PASSWORD	
SECURITY QUESTION	
ANSWER	
SECURITY QUESTION	
ANSWER	
SECURITY QUESTION	
ANSWER	

WEBSITE	
PURPOSE	
USERNAME	
PASSWORD	
SECURITY QUESTION	
ANSWER	
SECURITY QUESTION	
ANSWER	
SECURITY QUESTION	
ANSWER	

WEBSITE	
PURPOSE	
USERNAME	
PASSWORD	
SECURITY QUESTION	
ANSWER	
SECURITY QUESTION	
ANSWER	
SECURITY QUESTION	
ANSWER	

Online Passwords

WEBSITE

PURPOSE

USERNAME

PASSWORD

SECURITY QUESTION

ANSWER

SECURITY QUESTION

ANSWER

SECURITY QUESTION

ANSWER

WEBSITE

PURPOSE

USERNAME

PASSWORD

SECURITY QUESTION

ANSWER

SECURITY QUESTION

ANSWER

SECURITY QUESTION

ANSWER

WEBSITE

PURPOSE

USERNAME

PASSWORD

SECURITY QUESTION

ANSWER

SECURITY QUESTION

ANSWER

SECURITY QUESTION

ANSWER

Online Passwords

WEBSITE	
PURPOSE	
USERNAME	
PASSWORD	
SECURITY QUESTION	
ANSWER	
SECURITY QUESTION	
ANSWER	
SECURITY QUESTION	
ANSWER	

WEBSITE	
PURPOSE	
USERNAME	
PASSWORD	
SECURITY QUESTION	
ANSWER	
SECURITY QUESTION	
ANSWER	
SECURITY QUESTION	
ANSWER	

WEBSITE	
PURPOSE	
USERNAME	
PASSWORD	
SECURITY QUESTION	
ANSWER	
SECURITY QUESTION	
ANSWER	
SECURITY QUESTION	
ANSWER	

Online Passwords

WEBSITE
PURPOSE
USERNAME
PASSWORD
SECURITY QUESTION
ANSWER
SECURITY QUESTION
ANSWER
SECURITY QUESTION
ANSWER

WEBSITE
PURPOSE
USERNAME
PASSWORD
SECURITY QUESTION
ANSWER
SECURITY QUESTION
ANSWER
SECURITY QUESTION
ANSWER

WEBSITE
PURPOSE
USERNAME
PASSWORD
SECURITY QUESTION
ANSWER
SECURITY QUESTION
ANSWER
SECURITY QUESTION
ANSWER

Online Passwords

WEBSITE	
PURPOSE	
USERNAME	
PASSWORD	
SECURITY QUESTION	
ANSWER	
SECURITY QUESTION	
ANSWER	
SECURITY QUESTION	
ANSWER	

WEBSITE	
PURPOSE	
USERNAME	
PASSWORD	
SECURITY QUESTION	
ANSWER	
SECURITY QUESTION	
ANSWER	
SECURITY QUESTION	
ANSWER	

WEBSITE	
PURPOSE	
USERNAME	
PASSWORD	
SECURITY QUESTION	
ANSWER	
SECURITY QUESTION	
ANSWER	
SECURITY QUESTION	
ANSWER	

Online Passwords

WEBSITE	
PURPOSE	
USERNAME	
PASSWORD	
SECURITY QUESTION	
ANSWER	
SECURITY QUESTION	
ANSWER	
SECURITY QUESTION	
ANSWER	

WEBSITE	
PURPOSE	
USERNAME	
PASSWORD	
SECURITY QUESTION	
ANSWER	
SECURITY QUESTION	
ANSWER	
SECURITY QUESTION	
ANSWER	

WEBSITE	
PURPOSE	
USERNAME	
PASSWORD	
SECURITY QUESTION	
ANSWER	
SECURITY QUESTION	
ANSWER	
SECURITY QUESTION	
ANSWER	

Online Passwords

WEBSITE	
PURPOSE	
USERNAME	
PASSWORD	
SECURITY QUESTION	
ANSWER	
SECURITY QUESTION	
ANSWER	
SECURITY QUESTION	
ANSWER	

WEBSITE	
PURPOSE	
USERNAME	
PASSWORD	
SECURITY QUESTION	
ANSWER	
SECURITY QUESTION	
ANSWER	
SECURITY QUESTION	
ANSWER	

WEBSITE	
PURPOSE	
USERNAME	
PASSWORD	
SECURITY QUESTION	
ANSWER	
SECURITY QUESTION	
ANSWER	
SECURITY QUESTION	
ANSWER	

Online Passwords

WEBSITE
PURPOSE
USERNAME
PASSWORD
SECURITY QUESTION
ANSWER
SECURITY QUESTION
ANSWER
SECURITY QUESTION
ANSWER

WEBSITE
PURPOSE
USERNAME
PASSWORD
SECURITY QUESTION
ANSWER
SECURITY QUESTION
ANSWER
SECURITY QUESTION
ANSWER

WEBSITE
PURPOSE
USERNAME
PASSWORD
SECURITY QUESTION
ANSWER
SECURITY QUESTION
ANSWER
SECURITY QUESTION
ANSWER

Online Passwords

WEBSITE	
PURPOSE	
USERNAME	
PASSWORD	
SECURITY QUESTION	
ANSWER	
SECURITY QUESTION	
ANSWER	
SECURITY QUESTION	
ANSWER	

WEBSITE	
PURPOSE	
USERNAME	
PASSWORD	
SECURITY QUESTION	
ANSWER	
SECURITY QUESTION	
ANSWER	
SECURITY QUESTION	
ANSWER	

WEBSITE	
PURPOSE	
USERNAME	
PASSWORD	
SECURITY QUESTION	
ANSWER	
SECURITY QUESTION	
ANSWER	
SECURITY QUESTION	
ANSWER	

Online Passwords

WEBSITE
PURPOSE
USERNAME
PASSWORD
SECURITY QUESTION
ANSWER
SECURITY QUESTION
ANSWER
SECURITY QUESTION
ANSWER

WEBSITE
PURPOSE
USERNAME
PASSWORD
SECURITY QUESTION
ANSWER
SECURITY QUESTION
ANSWER
SECURITY QUESTION
ANSWER

WEBSITE
PURPOSE
USERNAME
PASSWORD
SECURITY QUESTION
ANSWER
SECURITY QUESTION
ANSWER
SECURITY QUESTION
ANSWER

Credit Cards

❏ VISA	❏ MASTERCARD	❏ AMEX	❏ DISCOVER	❏ OTHER	
CARD NUMBER					
EXPIRATION DATE			CVV		
PHONE					
WEBSITE					
USERNAME					
PASSWORD					❏ SEE PASSWORDS

❏ VISA	❏ MASTERCARD	❏ AMEX	❏ DISCOVER	❏ OTHER	
CARD NUMBER					
EXPIRATION DATE			CVV		
PHONE					
WEBSITE					
USERNAME					
PASSWORD					❏ SEE PASSWORDS

❏ VISA	❏ MASTERCARD	❏ AMEX	❏ DISCOVER	❏ OTHER	
CARD NUMBER					
EXPIRATION DATE			CVV		
PHONE					
WEBSITE					
USERNAME					
PASSWORD					❏ SEE PASSWORDS

❏ VISA	❏ MASTERCARD	❏ AMEX	❏ DISCOVER	❏ OTHER	
CARD NUMBER					
EXPIRATION DATE			CVV		
PHONE					
WEBSITE					
USERNAME					
PASSWORD					❏ SEE PASSWORDS

Credit Cards

❏ VISA   ❏ MASTERCARD   ❏ AMEX   ❏ DISCOVER   ❏ OTHER

CARD NUMBER	
EXPIRATION DATE	CVV
PHONE	
WEBSITE	
USERNAME	
PASSWORD	❏ SEE PASSWORDS

❏ VISA   ❏ MASTERCARD   ❏ AMEX   ❏ DISCOVER   ❏ OTHER

CARD NUMBER	
EXPIRATION DATE	CVV
PHONE	
WEBSITE	
USERNAME	
PASSWORD	❏ SEE PASSWORDS

❏ VISA   ❏ MASTERCARD   ❏ AMEX   ❏ DISCOVER   ❏ OTHER

CARD NUMBER	
EXPIRATION DATE	CVV
PHONE	
WEBSITE	
USERNAME	
PASSWORD	❏ SEE PASSWORDS

❏ VISA   ❏ MASTERCARD   ❏ AMEX   ❏ DISCOVER   ❏ OTHER

CARD NUMBER	
EXPIRATION DATE	CVV
PHONE	
WEBSITE	
USERNAME	
PASSWORD	❏ SEE PASSWORDS

Credit Cards

❑ VISA	❑ MASTERCARD	❑ AMEX	❑ DISCOVER	❑ OTHER	
CARD NUMBER					
EXPIRATION DATE			CVV		
PHONE					
WEBSITE					
USERNAME					
PASSWORD					❑ SEE PASSWORDS

❑ VISA	❑ MASTERCARD	❑ AMEX	❑ DISCOVER	❑ OTHER	
CARD NUMBER					
EXPIRATION DATE			CVV		
PHONE					
WEBSITE					
USERNAME					
PASSWORD					❑ SEE PASSWORDS

❑ VISA	❑ MASTERCARD	❑ AMEX	❑ DISCOVER	❑ OTHER	
CARD NUMBER					
EXPIRATION DATE			CVV		
PHONE					
WEBSITE					
USERNAME					
PASSWORD					❑ SEE PASSWORDS

❑ VISA	❑ MASTERCARD	❑ AMEX	❑ DISCOVER	❑ OTHER	
CARD NUMBER					
EXPIRATION DATE			CVV		
PHONE					
WEBSITE					
USERNAME					
PASSWORD					❑ SEE PASSWORDS

Credit Cards

❏ VISA ❏ MASTERCARD ❏ AMEX ❏ DISCOVER ❏ OTHER

CARD NUMBER

EXPIRATION DATE

CVV

PHONE

WEBSITE

USERNAME

PASSWORD

❏ SEE PASSWORDS

❏ VISA ❏ MASTERCARD ❏ AMEX ❏ DISCOVER ❏ OTHER

CARD NUMBER

EXPIRATION DATE

CVV

PHONE

WEBSITE

USERNAME

PASSWORD

❏ SEE PASSWORDS

❏ VISA ❏ MASTERCARD ❏ AMEX ❏ DISCOVER ❏ OTHER

CARD NUMBER

EXPIRATION DATE

CVV

PHONE

WEBSITE

USERNAME

PASSWORD

❏ SEE PASSWORDS

❏ VISA ❏ MASTERCARD ❏ AMEX ❏ DISCOVER ❏ OTHER

CARD NUMBER

EXPIRATION DATE

CVV

PHONE

WEBSITE

USERNAME

PASSWORD

❏ SEE PASSWORDS

Financial Institutions

❏ *CHECKING*   ❏ *SAVINGS*   ❏ *MONEY MARKET*   ❏ *INVESTMENT*   ❏ *OTHER*

BANK		
CONTACT		
PHONE		
STREET ADDRESS		
CITY	*STATE*	*ZIP*
ACCOUNT #		
WEBSITE		
USERNAME		
PASSWORD		❏ *SEE PASSWORDS*

❏ *CHECKING*   ❏ *SAVINGS*   ❏ *PROPERTY LOAN*   ❏ *PERSONAL LOAN*   ❏ *OTHER*

BANK		
CONTACT		
PHONE		
STREET ADDRESS		
CITY	*STATE*	*ZIP*
ACCOUNT #		
WEBSITE		
USERNAME		
PASSWORD		❏ *SEE PASSWORDS*

❏ *CHECKING*   ❏ *SAVINGS*   ❏ *PROPERTY LOAN*   ❏ *PERSONAL LOAN*   ❏ *OTHER*

BANK		
CONTACT		
PHONE		
STREET ADDRESS		
CITY	*STATE*	*ZIP*
ACCOUNT #		
WEBSITE		
USERNAME		
PASSWORD		❏ *SEE PASSWORDS*

Financial Institutions

❑ *CHECKING*   ❑ *SAVINGS*   ❑ *MONEY MARKET*   ❑ *INVESTMENT*   ❑ *OTHER*

BANK	
CONTACT	
PHONE	
STREET ADDRESS	
CITY	*STATE* *ZIP*
ACCOUNT #	
WEBSITE	
USERNAME	
PASSWORD	❑ *SEE PASSWORDS*

❑ *CHECKING*   ❑ *SAVINGS*   ❑ *PROPERTY LOAN*   ❑ *PERSONAL LOAN*   ❑ *OTHER*

BANK	
CONTACT	
PHONE	
STREET ADDRESS	
CITY	*STATE* *ZIP*
ACCOUNT #	
WEBSITE	
USERNAME	
PASSWORD	❑ *SEE PASSWORDS*

❑ *CHECKING*   ❑ *SAVINGS*   ❑ *PROPERTY LOAN*   ❑ *PERSONAL LOAN*   ❑ *OTHER*

BANK	
CONTACT	
PHONE	
STREET ADDRESS	
CITY	*STATE* *ZIP*
ACCOUNT #	
WEBSITE	
USERNAME	
PASSWORD	❑ *SEE PASSWORDS*

Financial Institutions

❑ *CHECKING* ❑ *SAVINGS* ❑ *MONEY MARKET* ❑ *INVESTMENT* ❑ *OTHER*		
BANK		
CONTACT		
PHONE		
STREET ADDRESS		
CITY	*STATE*	*ZIP*
ACCOUNT #		
WEBSITE		
USERNAME		
PASSWORD		❑ *SEE PASSWORDS*

❑ *CHECKING* ❑ *SAVINGS* ❑ *PROPERTY LOAN* ❑ *PERSONAL LOAN* ❑ *OTHER*		
BANK		
CONTACT		
PHONE		
STREET ADDRESS		
CITY	*STATE*	*ZIP*
ACCOUNT #		
WEBSITE		
USERNAME		
PASSWORD		❑ *SEE PASSWORDS*

❑ *CHECKING* ❑ *SAVINGS* ❑ *PROPERTY LOAN* ❑ *PERSONAL LOAN* ❑ *OTHER*		
BANK		
CONTACT		
PHONE		
STREET ADDRESS		
CITY	*STATE*	*ZIP*
ACCOUNT #		
WEBSITE		
USERNAME		
PASSWORD		❑ *SEE PASSWORDS*

Financial Institutions

❑ CHECKING ❑ SAVINGS ❑ MONEY MARKET ❑ INVESTMENT ❑ OTHER

BANK	
CONTACT	
PHONE	
STREET ADDRESS	
CITY	STATE ZIP
ACCOUNT #	
WEBSITE	
USERNAME	
PASSWORD	❑ SEE PASSWORDS

❑ CHECKING ❑ SAVINGS ❑ PROPERTY LOAN ❑ PERSONAL LOAN ❑ OTHER

BANK	
CONTACT	
PHONE	
STREET ADDRESS	
CITY	STATE ZIP
ACCOUNT #	
WEBSITE	
USERNAME	
PASSWORD	❑ SEE PASSWORDS

❑ CHECKING ❑ SAVINGS ❑ PROPERTY LOAN ❑ PERSONAL LOAN ❑ OTHER

BANK	
CONTACT	
PHONE	
STREET ADDRESS	
CITY	STATE ZIP
ACCOUNT #	
WEBSITE	
USERNAME	
PASSWORD	❑ SEE PASSWORDS

Investment Accounts

ACCOUNT TYPE		
COMPANY		
CONTACT		
PHONE		
STREET ADDRESS		
CITY	STATE	ZIP
ACCOUNT #		
WEBSITE		
USERNAME		
PASSWORD		❑ SEE PASSWORDS

ACCOUNT TYPE		
COMPANY		
CONTACT		
PHONE		
STREET ADDRESS		
CITY	STATE	ZIP
ACCOUNT #		
WEBSITE		
USERNAME		
PASSWORD		❑ SEE PASSWORDS

ACCOUNT TYPE		
COMPANY		
CONTACT		
PHONE		
STREET ADDRESS		
CITY	STATE	ZIP
ACCOUNT #		
WEBSITE		
USERNAME		
PASSWORD		❑ SEE PASSWORDS

Investment Accounts

ACCOUNT TYPE		
COMPANY		
CONTACT		
PHONE		
STREET ADDRESS		
CITY	STATE	ZIP
ACCOUNT #		
WEBSITE		
USERNAME		
PASSWORD		❏ SEE PASSWORDS

ACCOUNT TYPE		
COMPANY		
CONTACT		
PHONE		
STREET ADDRESS		
CITY	STATE	ZIP
ACCOUNT #		
WEBSITE		
USERNAME		
PASSWORD		❏ SEE PASSWORDS

ACCOUNT TYPE		
COMPANY		
CONTACT		
PHONE		
STREET ADDRESS		
CITY	STATE	ZIP
ACCOUNT #		
WEBSITE		
USERNAME		
PASSWORD		❏ SEE PASSWORDS

Investment Accounts

ACCOUNT TYPE	
COMPANY	
CONTACT	
PHONE	
STREET ADDRESS	
CITY	*STATE* *ZIP*
ACCOUNT #	
WEBSITE	
USERNAME	
PASSWORD	❏ *SEE PASSWORDS*

ACCOUNT TYPE	
COMPANY	
CONTACT	
PHONE	
STREET ADDRESS	
CITY	*STATE* *ZIP*
ACCOUNT #	
WEBSITE	
USERNAME	
PASSWORD	❏ *SEE PASSWORDS*

ACCOUNT TYPE	
COMPANY	
CONTACT	
PHONE	
STREET ADDRESS	
CITY	*STATE* *ZIP*
ACCOUNT #	
WEBSITE	
USERNAME	
PASSWORD	❏ *SEE PASSWORDS*

Investment Accounts

ACCOUNT TYPE	
COMPANY	
CONTACT	
PHONE	
STREET ADDRESS	
CITY	STATE ZIP
ACCOUNT #	
WEBSITE	
USERNAME	
PASSWORD	❏ SEE PASSWORDS

ACCOUNT TYPE	
COMPANY	
CONTACT	
PHONE	
STREET ADDRESS	
CITY	STATE ZIP
ACCOUNT #	
WEBSITE	
USERNAME	
PASSWORD	❏ SEE PASSWORDS

ACCOUNT TYPE	
COMPANY	
CONTACT	
PHONE	
STREET ADDRESS	
CITY	STATE ZIP
ACCOUNT #	
WEBSITE	
USERNAME	
PASSWORD	❏ SEE PASSWORDS

Retirement Accounts

ACCOUNT TYPE		
COMPANY		
CONTACT		
PHONE		
STREET ADDRESS		
CITY	STATE	ZIP
ACCOUNT #		
WEBSITE		
USERNAME		
PASSWORD		❏ SEE PASSWORDS

ACCOUNT TYPE		
COMPANY		
CONTACT		
PHONE		
STREET ADDRESS		
CITY	STATE	ZIP
ACCOUNT #		
WEBSITE		
USERNAME		
PASSWORD		❏ SEE PASSWORDS

ACCOUNT TYPE		
COMPANY		
CONTACT		
PHONE		
STREET ADDRESS		
CITY	STATE	ZIP
ACCOUNT #		
WEBSITE		
USERNAME		
PASSWORD		❏ SEE PASSWORDS

Retirement Accounts

ACCOUNT TYPE		
COMPANY		
CONTACT		
PHONE		
STREET ADDRESS		
CITY	STATE	ZIP
ACCOUNT #		
WEBSITE		
USERNAME		
PASSWORD		❏ SEE PASSWORDS

ACCOUNT TYPE		
COMPANY		
CONTACT		
PHONE		
STREET ADDRESS		
CITY	STATE	ZIP
ACCOUNT #		
WEBSITE		
USERNAME		
PASSWORD		❏ SEE PASSWORDS

ACCOUNT TYPE		
COMPANY		
CONTACT		
PHONE		
STREET ADDRESS		
CITY	STATE	ZIP
ACCOUNT #		
WEBSITE		
USERNAME		
PASSWORD		❏ SEE PASSWORDS

Retirement Accounts

ACCOUNT TYPE	
COMPANY	
CONTACT	
PHONE	
STREET ADDRESS	
CITY	STATE · ZIP
ACCOUNT #	
WEBSITE	
USERNAME	
PASSWORD	❑ SEE PASSWORDS

ACCOUNT TYPE	
COMPANY	
CONTACT	
PHONE	
STREET ADDRESS	
CITY	STATE · ZIP
ACCOUNT #	
WEBSITE	
USERNAME	
PASSWORD	❑ SEE PASSWORDS

ACCOUNT TYPE	
COMPANY	
CONTACT	
PHONE	
STREET ADDRESS	
CITY	STATE · ZIP
ACCOUNT #	
WEBSITE	
USERNAME	
PASSWORD	❑ SEE PASSWORDS

Retirement Accounts

ACCOUNT TYPE		
COMPANY		
CONTACT		
PHONE		
STREET ADDRESS		
CITY	*STATE*	*ZIP*
ACCOUNT #		
WEBSITE		
USERNAME		
PASSWORD		❏ *SEE PASSWORDS*

ACCOUNT TYPE		
COMPANY		
CONTACT		
PHONE		
STREET ADDRESS		
CITY	*STATE*	*ZIP*
ACCOUNT #		
WEBSITE		
USERNAME		
PASSWORD		❏ *SEE PASSWORDS*

ACCOUNT TYPE		
COMPANY		
CONTACT		
PHONE		
STREET ADDRESS		
CITY	*STATE*	*ZIP*
ACCOUNT #		
WEBSITE		
USERNAME		
PASSWORD		❏ *SEE PASSWORDS*

Insurance Policies

INSURANCE TYPE	
COMPANY	
CONTACT	
PHONE	
STREET ADDRESS	
CITY	STATE ZIP
ACCOUNT #	
WEBSITE	
USERNAME	
PASSWORD	❑ SEE PASSWORDS

INSURANCE TYPE	
COMPANY	
CONTACT	
PHONE	
STREET ADDRESS	
CITY	STATE ZIP
ACCOUNT #	
WEBSITE	
USERNAME	
PASSWORD	❑ SEE PASSWORDS

INSURANCE TYPE	
COMPANY	
CONTACT	
PHONE	
STREET ADDRESS	
CITY	STATE ZIP
ACCOUNT #	
WEBSITE	
USERNAME	
PASSWORD	❑ SEE PASSWORDS

Insurance Policies

INSURANCE TYPE		
COMPANY		
CONTACT		
PHONE		
STREET ADDRESS		
CITY	STATE	ZIP
ACCOUNT #		
WEBSITE		
USERNAME		
PASSWORD		❏ SEE PASSWORDS

INSURANCE TYPE		
COMPANY		
CONTACT		
PHONE		
STREET ADDRESS		
CITY	STATE	ZIP
ACCOUNT #		
WEBSITE		
USERNAME		
PASSWORD		❏ SEE PASSWORDS

INSURANCE TYPE		
COMPANY		
CONTACT		
PHONE		
STREET ADDRESS		
CITY	STATE	ZIP
ACCOUNT #		
WEBSITE		
USERNAME		
PASSWORD		❏ SEE PASSWORDS

Insurance Policies

INSURANCE TYPE			
COMPANY			
CONTACT			
PHONE			
STREET ADDRESS			
CITY	*STATE*	*ZIP*	
ACCOUNT #			
WEBSITE			
USERNAME			
PASSWORD			❏ *SEE PASSWORDS*

INSURANCE TYPE			
COMPANY			
CONTACT			
PHONE			
STREET ADDRESS			
CITY	*STATE*	*ZIP*	
ACCOUNT #			
WEBSITE			
USERNAME			
PASSWORD			❏ *SEE PASSWORDS*

INSURANCE TYPE			
COMPANY			
CONTACT			
PHONE			
STREET ADDRESS			
CITY	*STATE*	*ZIP*	
ACCOUNT #			
WEBSITE			
USERNAME			
PASSWORD			❏ *SEE PASSWORDS*

Insurance Policies

INSURANCE TYPE	
COMPANY	
CONTACT	
PHONE	
STREET ADDRESS	
CITY	*STATE* *ZIP*
ACCOUNT #	
WEBSITE	
USERNAME	
PASSWORD	❑ *SEE PASSWORDS*

INSURANCE TYPE	
COMPANY	
CONTACT	
PHONE	
STREET ADDRESS	
CITY	*STATE* *ZIP*
ACCOUNT #	
WEBSITE	
USERNAME	
PASSWORD	❑ *SEE PASSWORDS*

INSURANCE TYPE	
COMPANY	
CONTACT	
PHONE	
STREET ADDRESS	
CITY	*STATE* *ZIP*
ACCOUNT #	
WEBSITE	
USERNAME	
PASSWORD	❑ *SEE PASSWORDS*

Active Loans and Debt

❏ CREDIT CARD ❏ PROPERTY LOAN ❏ PERSONAL LOAN ❏ OTHER		
BANK		
CONTACT		
PHONE		
STREET ADDRESS		
CITY	STATE	ZIP
ACCOUNT #		❏ LOAN PAID OFF
WEBSITE		
USERNAME		
PASSWORD		❏ SEE PASSWORDS

❏ CREDIT CARD ❏ PROPERTY LOAN ❏ PERSONAL LOAN ❏ OTHER		
BANK		
CONTACT		
PHONE		
STREET ADDRESS		
CITY	STATE	ZIP
ACCOUNT #		❏ LOAN PAID OFF
WEBSITE		
USERNAME		
PASSWORD		❏ SEE PASSWORDS

❏ CREDIT CARD ❏ PROPERTY LOAN ❏ PERSONAL LOAN ❏ OTHER		
BANK		
CONTACT		
PHONE		
STREET ADDRESS		
CITY	STATE	ZIP
ACCOUNT #		❏ LOAN PAID OFF
WEBSITE		
USERNAME		
PASSWORD		❏ SEE PASSWORDS

Active Loans and Debt

❏ *CREDIT CARD*   ❏ *PROPERTY LOAN*   ❏ *PERSONAL LOAN*   ❏ *OTHER*

BANK

CONTACT

PHONE

STREET ADDRESS

CITY   *STATE*   *ZIP*

ACCOUNT #   ❏ *LOAN PAID OFF*

WEBSITE

USERNAME

PASSWORD   ❏ *SEE PASSWORDS*

❏ *CREDIT CARD*   ❏ *PROPERTY LOAN*   ❏ *PERSONAL LOAN*   ❏ *OTHER*

BANK

CONTACT

PHONE

STREET ADDRESS

CITY   *STATE*   *ZIP*

ACCOUNT #   ❏ *LOAN PAID OFF*

WEBSITE

USERNAME

PASSWORD   ❏ *SEE PASSWORDS*

❏ *CREDIT CARD*   ❏ *PROPERTY LOAN*   ❏ *PERSONAL LOAN*   ❏ *OTHER*

BANK

CONTACT

PHONE

STREET ADDRESS

CITY   *STATE*   *ZIP*

ACCOUNT #   ❏ *LOAN PAID OFF*

WEBSITE

USERNAME

PASSWORD   ❏ *SEE PASSWORDS*

Active Loans and Debt

❑ *CREDIT CARD*   ❑ *PROPERTY LOAN*   ❑ *PERSONAL LOAN*   ❑ *OTHER*

BANK		
CONTACT		
PHONE		
STREET ADDRESS		
CITY	*STATE*	*ZIP*
ACCOUNT #		❑ *LOAN PAID OFF*
WEBSITE		
USERNAME		
PASSWORD		❑ *SEE PASSWORDS*

❑ *CREDIT CARD*   ❑ *PROPERTY LOAN*   ❑ *PERSONAL LOAN*   ❑ *OTHER*

BANK		
CONTACT		
PHONE		
STREET ADDRESS		
CITY	*STATE*	*ZIP*
ACCOUNT #		❑ *LOAN PAID OFF*
WEBSITE		
USERNAME		
PASSWORD		❑ *SEE PASSWORDS*

❑ *CREDIT CARD*   ❑ *PROPERTY LOAN*   ❑ *PERSONAL LOAN*   ❑ *OTHER*

BANK		
CONTACT		
PHONE		
STREET ADDRESS		
CITY	*STATE*	*ZIP*
ACCOUNT #		❑ *LOAN PAID OFF*
WEBSITE		
USERNAME		
PASSWORD		❑ *SEE PASSWORDS*

Active Loans and Debt

❑ *CREDIT CARD*   ❑ *PROPERTY LOAN*   ❑ *PERSONAL LOAN*   ❑ *OTHER*

BANK		
CONTACT		
PHONE		
STREET ADDRESS		
CITY	*STATE*	*ZIP*
ACCOUNT #		❑ *LOAN PAID OFF*
WEBSITE		
USERNAME		
PASSWORD		❑ *SEE PASSWORDS*

❑ *CREDIT CARD*   ❑ *PROPERTY LOAN*   ❑ *PERSONAL LOAN*   ❑ *OTHER*

BANK		
CONTACT		
PHONE		
STREET ADDRESS		
CITY	*STATE*	*ZIP*
ACCOUNT #		❑ *LOAN PAID OFF*
WEBSITE		
USERNAME		
PASSWORD		❑ *SEE PASSWORDS*

❑ *CREDIT CARD*   ❑ *PROPERTY LOAN*   ❑ *PERSONAL LOAN*   ❑ *OTHER*

BANK		
CONTACT		
PHONE		
STREET ADDRESS		
CITY	*STATE*	*ZIP*
ACCOUNT #		❑ *LOAN PAID OFF*
WEBSITE		
USERNAME		
PASSWORD		❑ *SEE PASSWORDS*

Active Loans and Debt

❏ CREDIT CARD   ❏ PROPERTY LOAN   ❏ PERSONAL LOAN   ❏ OTHER

BANK		
CONTACT		
PHONE		
STREET ADDRESS		
CITY	STATE	ZIP
ACCOUNT #		❏ LOAN PAID OFF
WEBSITE		
USERNAME		
PASSWORD		❏ SEE PASSWORDS

❏ CREDIT CARD   ❏ PROPERTY LOAN   ❏ PERSONAL LOAN   ❏ OTHER

BANK		
CONTACT		
PHONE		
STREET ADDRESS		
CITY	STATE	ZIP
ACCOUNT #		❏ LOAN PAID OFF
WEBSITE		
USERNAME		
PASSWORD		❏ SEE PASSWORDS

❏ CREDIT CARD   ❏ PROPERTY LOAN   ❏ PERSONAL LOAN   ❏ OTHER

BANK		
CONTACT		
PHONE		
STREET ADDRESS		
CITY	STATE	ZIP
ACCOUNT #		❏ LOAN PAID OFF
WEBSITE		
USERNAME		
PASSWORD		❏ SEE PASSWORDS

Active Loans and Debt

❑ *CREDIT CARD*   ❑ *PROPERTY LOAN*   ❑ *PERSONAL LOAN*   ❑ *OTHER*

BANK

CONTACT

PHONE

STREET ADDRESS

CITY   *STATE*   *ZIP*

ACCOUNT #
                                                              ❑ *LOAN PAID OFF*

WEBSITE

USERNAME

PASSWORD
                                                              ❑ *SEE PASSWORDS*

❑ *CREDIT CARD*   ❑ *PROPERTY LOAN*   ❑ *PERSONAL LOAN*   ❑ *OTHER*

BANK

CONTACT

PHONE

STREET ADDRESS

CITY   *STATE*   *ZIP*

ACCOUNT #
                                                              ❑ *LOAN PAID OFF*

WEBSITE

USERNAME

PASSWORD
                                                              ❑ *SEE PASSWORDS*

❑ *CREDIT CARD*   ❑ *PROPERTY LOAN*   ❑ *PERSONAL LOAN*   ❑ *OTHER*

BANK

CONTACT

PHONE

STREET ADDRESS

CITY   *STATE*   *ZIP*

ACCOUNT #
                                                              ❑ *LOAN PAID OFF*

WEBSITE

USERNAME

PASSWORD
                                                              ❑ *SEE PASSWORDS*

Active Loans and Debt

❏ CREDIT CARD	❏ PROPERTY LOAN	❏ PERSONAL LOAN	❏ OTHER

BANK		
CONTACT		
PHONE		
STREET ADDRESS		
CITY	STATE	ZIP
ACCOUNT #		❏ LOAN PAID OFF
WEBSITE		
USERNAME		
PASSWORD		❏ SEE PASSWORDS

❏ CREDIT CARD	❏ PROPERTY LOAN	❏ PERSONAL LOAN	❏ OTHER

BANK		
CONTACT		
PHONE		
STREET ADDRESS		
CITY	STATE	ZIP
ACCOUNT #		❏ LOAN PAID OFF
WEBSITE		
USERNAME		
PASSWORD		❏ SEE PASSWORDS

❏ CREDIT CARD	❏ PROPERTY LOAN	❏ PERSONAL LOAN	❏ OTHER

BANK		
CONTACT		
PHONE		
STREET ADDRESS		
CITY	STATE	ZIP
ACCOUNT #		❏ LOAN PAID OFF
WEBSITE		
USERNAME		
PASSWORD		❏ SEE PASSWORDS

Active Loans and Debt

❏ *CREDIT CARD*   ❏ *PROPERTY LOAN*   ❏ *PERSONAL LOAN*   ❏ *OTHER*

BANK

CONTACT

PHONE

STREET ADDRESS

CITY   *STATE*   *ZIP*

ACCOUNT #   ❏ *LOAN PAID OFF*

WEBSITE

USERNAME

PASSWORD   ❏ *SEE PASSWORDS*

❏ *CREDIT CARD*   ❏ *PROPERTY LOAN*   ❏ *PERSONAL LOAN*   ❏ *OTHER*

BANK

CONTACT

PHONE

STREET ADDRESS

CITY   *STATE*   *ZIP*

ACCOUNT #   ❏ *LOAN PAID OFF*

WEBSITE

USERNAME

PASSWORD   ❏ *SEE PASSWORDS*

❏ *CREDIT CARD*   ❏ *PROPERTY LOAN*   ❏ *PERSONAL LOAN*   ❏ *OTHER*

BANK

CONTACT

PHONE

STREET ADDRESS

CITY   *STATE*   *ZIP*

ACCOUNT #   ❏ *LOAN PAID OFF*

WEBSITE

USERNAME

PASSWORD   ❏ *SEE PASSWORDS*

Monthly Bills

COMPANY

MAILING ADDRESS

CITY   STATE   ZIP

ACCOUNT #   AMOUNT $

WEBSITE

USERNAME

PASSWORD   ❏ SEE PASSWORDS

COMPANY

MAILING ADDRESS

CITY   STATE   ZIP

ACCOUNT #   AMOUNT $

WEBSITE

USERNAME

PASSWORD   ❏ SEE PASSWORDS

COMPANY

MAILING ADDRESS

CITY   STATE   ZIP

ACCOUNT #   AMOUNT $

WEBSITE

USERNAME

PASSWORD   ❏ SEE PASSWORDS

COMPANY

MAILING ADDRESS

CITY   STATE   ZIP

ACCOUNT #   AMOUNT $

WEBSITE

USERNAME

PASSWORD   ❏ SEE PASSWORDS

Monthly Bills

COMPANY

MAILING ADDRESS

CITY   STATE   ZIP

ACCOUNT #   AMOUNT $

WEBSITE

USERNAME

PASSWORD   ❑ SEE PASSWORDS

COMPANY

MAILING ADDRESS

CITY   STATE   ZIP

ACCOUNT #   AMOUNT $

WEBSITE

USERNAME

PASSWORD   ❑ SEE PASSWORDS

COMPANY

MAILING ADDRESS

CITY   STATE   ZIP

ACCOUNT #   AMOUNT $

WEBSITE

USERNAME

PASSWORD   ❑ SEE PASSWORDS

COMPANY

MAILING ADDRESS

CITY   STATE   ZIP

ACCOUNT #   AMOUNT $

WEBSITE

USERNAME

PASSWORD   ❑ SEE PASSWORDS

Monthly Bills

COMPANY		
MAILING ADDRESS		
CITY	STATE	ZIP
ACCOUNT #		AMOUNT $
WEBSITE		
USERNAME		
PASSWORD		❑ SEE PASSWORDS

COMPANY		
MAILING ADDRESS		
CITY	STATE	ZIP
ACCOUNT #		AMOUNT $
WEBSITE		
USERNAME		
PASSWORD		❑ SEE PASSWORDS

COMPANY		
MAILING ADDRESS		
CITY	STATE	ZIP
ACCOUNT #		AMOUNT $
WEBSITE		
USERNAME		
PASSWORD		❑ SEE PASSWORDS

COMPANY		
MAILING ADDRESS		
CITY	STATE	ZIP
ACCOUNT #		AMOUNT $
WEBSITE		
USERNAME		
PASSWORD		❑ SEE PASSWORDS

Monthly Bills

COMPANY		
MAILING ADDRESS		
CITY	STATE	ZIP
ACCOUNT #		AMOUNT $
WEBSITE		
USERNAME		
PASSWORD		❏ SEE PASSWORDS

COMPANY		
MAILING ADDRESS		
CITY	STATE	ZIP
ACCOUNT #		AMOUNT $
WEBSITE		
USERNAME		
PASSWORD		❏ SEE PASSWORDS

COMPANY		
MAILING ADDRESS		
CITY	STATE	ZIP
ACCOUNT #		AMOUNT $
WEBSITE		
USERNAME		
PASSWORD		❏ SEE PASSWORDS

COMPANY		
MAILING ADDRESS		
CITY	STATE	ZIP
ACCOUNT #		AMOUNT $
WEBSITE		
USERNAME		
PASSWORD		❏ SEE PASSWORDS

Monthly Bills

COMPANY	
MAILING ADDRESS	
CITY	STATE ZIP
ACCOUNT #	AMOUNT $
WEBSITE	
USERNAME	
PASSWORD	❏ SEE PASSWORDS

COMPANY	
MAILING ADDRESS	
CITY	STATE ZIP
ACCOUNT #	AMOUNT $
WEBSITE	
USERNAME	
PASSWORD	❏ SEE PASSWORDS

COMPANY	
MAILING ADDRESS	
CITY	STATE ZIP
ACCOUNT #	AMOUNT $
WEBSITE	
USERNAME	
PASSWORD	❏ SEE PASSWORDS

COMPANY	
MAILING ADDRESS	
CITY	STATE ZIP
ACCOUNT #	AMOUNT $
WEBSITE	
USERNAME	
PASSWORD	❏ SEE PASSWORDS

Monthly Bills

COMPANY

MAILING ADDRESS

CITY   STATE   ZIP

ACCOUNT #   AMOUNT $

WEBSITE

USERNAME

PASSWORD   ❏ SEE PASSWORDS

COMPANY

MAILING ADDRESS

CITY   STATE   ZIP

ACCOUNT #   AMOUNT $

WEBSITE

USERNAME

PASSWORD   ❏ SEE PASSWORDS

COMPANY

MAILING ADDRESS

CITY   STATE   ZIP

ACCOUNT #   AMOUNT $

WEBSITE

USERNAME

PASSWORD   ❏ SEE PASSWORDS

COMPANY

MAILING ADDRESS

CITY   STATE   ZIP

ACCOUNT #   AMOUNT $

WEBSITE

USERNAME

PASSWORD   ❏ SEE PASSWORDS

Monthly Bills

COMPANY		
MAILING ADDRESS		
CITY	STATE	ZIP
ACCOUNT #		AMOUNT $
WEBSITE		
USERNAME		
PASSWORD		❏ SEE PASSWORDS

COMPANY		
MAILING ADDRESS		
CITY	STATE	ZIP
ACCOUNT #		AMOUNT $
WEBSITE		
USERNAME		
PASSWORD		❏ SEE PASSWORDS

COMPANY		
MAILING ADDRESS		
CITY	STATE	ZIP
ACCOUNT #		AMOUNT $
WEBSITE		
USERNAME		
PASSWORD		❏ SEE PASSWORDS

COMPANY		
MAILING ADDRESS		
CITY	STATE	ZIP
ACCOUNT #		AMOUNT $
WEBSITE		
USERNAME		
PASSWORD		❏ SEE PASSWORDS

Monthly Bills

COMPANY

MAILING ADDRESS

CITY   STATE   ZIP

ACCOUNT #   AMOUNT $

WEBSITE

USERNAME

PASSWORD   ❏ SEE PASSWORDS

COMPANY

MAILING ADDRESS

CITY   STATE   ZIP

ACCOUNT #   AMOUNT $

WEBSITE

USERNAME

PASSWORD   ❏ SEE PASSWORDS

COMPANY

MAILING ADDRESS

CITY   STATE   ZIP

ACCOUNT #   AMOUNT $

WEBSITE

USERNAME

PASSWORD   ❏ SEE PASSWORDS

COMPANY

MAILING ADDRESS

CITY   STATE   ZIP

ACCOUNT #   AMOUNT $

WEBSITE

USERNAME

PASSWORD   ❏ SEE PASSWORDS

Monthly Bills

COMPANY		
MAILING ADDRESS		
CITY	STATE	ZIP
ACCOUNT #		AMOUNT $
WEBSITE		
USERNAME		
PASSWORD		❏ SEE PASSWORDS

COMPANY		
MAILING ADDRESS		
CITY	STATE	ZIP
ACCOUNT #		AMOUNT $
WEBSITE		
USERNAME		
PASSWORD		❏ SEE PASSWORDS

COMPANY		
MAILING ADDRESS		
CITY	STATE	ZIP
ACCOUNT #		AMOUNT $
WEBSITE		
USERNAME		
PASSWORD		❏ SEE PASSWORDS

COMPANY		
MAILING ADDRESS		
CITY	STATE	ZIP
ACCOUNT #		AMOUNT $
WEBSITE		
USERNAME		
PASSWORD		❏ SEE PASSWORDS

Monthly Bills

COMPANY	
MAILING ADDRESS	
CITY	STATE ZIP
ACCOUNT #	AMOUNT $
WEBSITE	
USERNAME	
PASSWORD	❏ SEE PASSWORDS

COMPANY	
MAILING ADDRESS	
CITY	STATE ZIP
ACCOUNT #	AMOUNT $
WEBSITE	
USERNAME	
PASSWORD	❏ SEE PASSWORDS

COMPANY	
MAILING ADDRESS	
CITY	STATE ZIP
ACCOUNT #	AMOUNT $
WEBSITE	
USERNAME	
PASSWORD	❏ SEE PASSWORDS

COMPANY	
MAILING ADDRESS	
CITY	STATE ZIP
ACCOUNT #	AMOUNT $
WEBSITE	
USERNAME	
PASSWORD	❏ SEE PASSWORDS

Monthly Bills

COMPANY		
MAILING ADDRESS		
CITY	STATE	ZIP
ACCOUNT #		AMOUNT $
WEBSITE		
USERNAME		
PASSWORD		❑ SEE PASSWORDS

COMPANY		
MAILING ADDRESS		
CITY	STATE	ZIP
ACCOUNT #		AMOUNT $
WEBSITE		
USERNAME		
PASSWORD		❑ SEE PASSWORDS

COMPANY		
MAILING ADDRESS		
CITY	STATE	ZIP
ACCOUNT #		AMOUNT $
WEBSITE		
USERNAME		
PASSWORD		❑ SEE PASSWORDS

COMPANY		
MAILING ADDRESS		
CITY	STATE	ZIP
ACCOUNT #		AMOUNT $
WEBSITE		
USERNAME		
PASSWORD		❑ SEE PASSWORDS

Monthly Bills

COMPANY

MAILING ADDRESS

CITY   STATE   ZIP

ACCOUNT #   AMOUNT $

WEBSITE

USERNAME

PASSWORD   ❏ SEE PASSWORDS

COMPANY

MAILING ADDRESS

CITY   STATE   ZIP

ACCOUNT #   AMOUNT $

WEBSITE

USERNAME

PASSWORD   ❏ SEE PASSWORDS

COMPANY

MAILING ADDRESS

CITY   STATE   ZIP

ACCOUNT #   AMOUNT $

WEBSITE

USERNAME

PASSWORD   ❏ SEE PASSWORDS

COMPANY

MAILING ADDRESS

CITY   STATE   ZIP

ACCOUNT #   AMOUNT $

WEBSITE

USERNAME

PASSWORD   ❏ SEE PASSWORDS

Important Contacts

ATTORNEY

NAME

PHONE

EMAIL

STREET ADDRESS

CITY   STATE   ZIP

NOTES

ACCOUNTANT

NAME

PHONE

EMAIL

STREET ADDRESS

CITY   STATE   ZIP

NOTES

BANKER

NAME

PHONE

EMAIL

STREET ADDRESS

CITY   STATE   ZIP

NOTES

INSURANCE AGENT

NAME

PHONE

EMAIL

STREET ADDRESS

CITY   STATE   ZIP

NOTES

Important Contacts

FINANCIAL PLANNER		
NAME		
PHONE		
EMAIL		
STREET ADDRESS		
CITY	STATE	ZIP
NOTES		

PRIMARY CARE PHYSICIAN		
NAME		
PHONE		
EMAIL		
STREET ADDRESS		
CITY	STATE	ZIP
NOTES		

CLERGY		
NAME		
PHONE		
EMAIL		
STREET ADDRESS		
CITY	STATE	ZIP
NOTES		

EXECUTOR		
NAME		
PHONE		
EMAIL		
STREET ADDRESS		
CITY	STATE	ZIP
NOTES		

Important Contacts

TRUSTEE		
NAME		
PHONE		
EMAIL		
STREET ADDRESS		
CITY	STATE	ZIP
NOTES		

GUARDIAN FOR CHILDREN		
NAME		
PHONE		
EMAIL		
STREET ADDRESS		
CITY	STATE	ZIP
NOTES		

EMPLOYER		
NAME		
PHONE		
EMAIL		
STREET ADDRESS		
CITY	STATE	ZIP
NOTES		

BOOKIE		
NAME		
PHONE		
EMAIL		
STREET ADDRESS		
CITY	STATE	ZIP
NOTES		

Important Contacts

RELATIONSHIP		
NAME		
PHONE		
EMAIL		
STREET ADDRESS		
CITY	STATE	ZIP
NOTES		

RELATIONSHIP		
NAME		
PHONE		
EMAIL		
STREET ADDRESS		
CITY	STATE	ZIP
NOTES		

RELATIONSHIP		
NAME		
PHONE		
EMAIL		
STREET ADDRESS		
CITY	STATE	ZIP
NOTES		

RELATIONSHIP		
NAME		
PHONE		
EMAIL		
STREET ADDRESS		
CITY	STATE	ZIP
NOTES		

Important Contacts

RELATIONSHIP			
NAME			
PHONE			
EMAIL			
STREET ADDRESS			
CITY		STATE	ZIP
NOTES			

RELATIONSHIP			
NAME			
PHONE			
EMAIL			
STREET ADDRESS			
CITY		STATE	ZIP
NOTES			

RELATIONSHIP			
NAME			
PHONE			
EMAIL			
STREET ADDRESS			
CITY		STATE	ZIP
NOTES			

RELATIONSHIP			
NAME			
PHONE			
EMAIL			
STREET ADDRESS			
CITY		STATE	ZIP
NOTES			

Important Contacts

RELATIONSHIP

NAME

PHONE

EMAIL

STREET ADDRESS

CITY   STATE   ZIP

NOTES

RELATIONSHIP

NAME

PHONE

EMAIL

STREET ADDRESS

CITY   STATE   ZIP

NOTES

RELATIONSHIP

NAME

PHONE

EMAIL

STREET ADDRESS

CITY   STATE   ZIP

NOTES

RELATIONSHIP

NAME

PHONE

EMAIL

STREET ADDRESS

CITY   STATE   ZIP

NOTES

Important Contacts

RELATIONSHIP			
NAME			
PHONE			
EMAIL			
STREET ADDRESS			
CITY	*STATE*	*ZIP*	
NOTES			

RELATIONSHIP			
NAME			
PHONE			
EMAIL			
STREET ADDRESS			
CITY	*STATE*	*ZIP*	
NOTES			

RELATIONSHIP			
NAME			
PHONE			
EMAIL			
STREET ADDRESS			
CITY	*STATE*	*ZIP*	
NOTES			

RELATIONSHIP			
NAME			
PHONE			
EMAIL			
STREET ADDRESS			
CITY	*STATE*	*ZIP*	
NOTES			

Important Contacts

RELATIONSHIP		
NAME		
PHONE		
EMAIL		
STREET ADDRESS		
CITY	*STATE*	*ZIP*
NOTES		

RELATIONSHIP		
NAME		
PHONE		
EMAIL		
STREET ADDRESS		
CITY	*STATE*	*ZIP*
NOTES		

RELATIONSHIP		
NAME		
PHONE		
EMAIL		
STREET ADDRESS		
CITY	*STATE*	*ZIP*
NOTES		

RELATIONSHIP		
NAME		
PHONE		
EMAIL		
STREET ADDRESS		
CITY	*STATE*	*ZIP*
NOTES		

Where to Find Things

HEALTH CARE DOCUMENTS	
HEALTH CARE PROXY	
FAMILY MEDICAL HISTORY	
DONOR INFORMATION	
FINANCIAL DOCUMENTS	
BANK STATEMENTS	
CREDIT CARD STATEMENTS	
INVESTMENT ACCOUNTS	
STOCK/BOND CERTIFICATES	
VETERANS' BENEFIT RECORDS	
DISABILITY DOCUMENTS	
INCOME STATEMENTS	
LOAN PAPERS	
TAX RETURNS	
HOUSEHOLD / PROPERTY / POSSESSIONS	
DEED AND ABSTRACT FOR HOME	
MORTGAGE DOCUMENTS	
TITLE INSURANCE POLICY	
RENTAL PROPERTY DOCUMENTS	
LIST OF POSSESSIONS	
VEHICLE TITLES	
AUTO INSURANCE POLICIES	
HOUSE KEYS	
VEHICLE KEYS	
RENTAL PROPERTY KEYS	
STORAGE UNIT KEYS	

Where to Find Things

INSURANCE POLICIES	
HEALTH INSURANCE	
LONG TERM HEALTH	
OTHER DEATH BENEFITS	
LIFE INSURANCE	
HOMEOWNERS / RENTERS POLICY	
PROPERTY / POSSESSION INVENTORY	
PROPERTY INSURANCE	
VEHICLE INSURANCE	

LEGAL INFORMATION	
MY WILL	
PARTNER'S WILL	
POWER OF ATTORNEY	
BIRTH CERTIFICATE	
ADOPTION RECORDS	
BUSINESS OWNERSHIP DOCUMENTS	
DIVORCE / SEPARATION PAPERS	
DRIVER'S LICENSE	
ID CARDS	
EMPLOYMENT INFORMATION	
MARRIAGE LICENSE	
MILITARY SERVICE PAPERS	
PASSPORT	
CITIZENSHIP / IMMIGRATION PAPERS	
SOCIAL SECURITY CARDS	

Where to Find Things

OTHER	
PASSWORD LIST	
MANUALS	
RECEIPTS	
WARRANTIES	
ALL THE STUFF YOU LEFT HERE WHEN YOU MOVED OUT	

Don't Look, Just Burn

FILES

COMPUTER FILES (OR MAYBE THE ENTIRE COMPUTER...)

DRAWERS

CABINETS

ROOMS

Important Computer Files

DESCRIPTION
FILE NAME
FILE LOCATION

DESCRIPTION
FILE NAME
FILE LOCATION

DESCRIPTION
FILE NAME
FILE LOCATION

DESCRIPTION
FILE NAME
FILE LOCATION

DESCRIPTION
FILE NAME
FILE LOCATION

DESCRIPTION
FILE NAME
FILE LOCATION

DESCRIPTION
FILE NAME
FILE LOCATION

DESCRIPTION
FILE NAME
FILE LOCATION

DESCRIPTION
FILE NAME
FILE LOCATION

Important Computer Files

DESCRIPTION

FILE NAME

FILE LOCATION

DESCRIPTION

FILE NAME

FILE LOCATION

DESCRIPTION

FILE NAME

FILE LOCATION

DESCRIPTION

FILE NAME

FILE LOCATION

DESCRIPTION

FILE NAME

FILE LOCATION

DESCRIPTION

FILE NAME

FILE LOCATION

DESCRIPTION

FILE NAME

FILE LOCATION

DESCRIPTION

FILE NAME

FILE LOCATION

DESCRIPTION

FILE NAME

FILE LOCATION

Keepsake Details

ITEM DESCRIPTION

VALUE

DATE ACQUIRED

HISTORY / BACKGROUND

ITEM DESCRIPTION

VALUE

DATE ACQUIRED

HISTORY / BACKGROUND

ITEM DESCRIPTION

VALUE

DATE ACQUIRED

HISTORY / BACKGROUND

Keepsake Details

ITEM DESCRIPTION

VALUE

DATE ACQUIRED

HISTORY / BACKGROUND

ITEM DESCRIPTION

VALUE

DATE ACQUIRED

HISTORY / BACKGROUND

ITEM DESCRIPTION

VALUE

DATE ACQUIRED

HISTORY / BACKGROUND

Keepsake Details

ITEM DESCRIPTION

VALUE

DATE ACQUIRED

HISTORY / BACKGROUND

ITEM DESCRIPTION

VALUE

DATE ACQUIRED

HISTORY / BACKGROUND

ITEM DESCRIPTION

VALUE

DATE ACQUIRED

HISTORY / BACKGROUND

Keepsake Details

ITEM DESCRIPTION

VALUE

DATE ACQUIRED

HISTORY / BACKGROUND

ITEM DESCRIPTION

VALUE

DATE ACQUIRED

HISTORY / BACKGROUND

ITEM DESCRIPTION

VALUE

DATE ACQUIRED

HISTORY / BACKGROUND

Keepsake Details

ITEM DESCRIPTION

VALUE

DATE ACQUIRED

HISTORY / BACKGROUND

ITEM DESCRIPTION

VALUE

DATE ACQUIRED

HISTORY / BACKGROUND

ITEM DESCRIPTION

VALUE

DATE ACQUIRED

HISTORY / BACKGROUND

Keepsake Details

ITEM DESCRIPTION

VALUE

DATE ACQUIRED

HISTORY / BACKGROUND

ITEM DESCRIPTION

VALUE

DATE ACQUIRED

HISTORY / BACKGROUND

ITEM DESCRIPTION

VALUE

DATE ACQUIRED

HISTORY / BACKGROUND

Photograph Details

PHOTOGRAPH DESCRIPTION

SUBJECTS

DATE TAKEN

LOCATION

HISTORY / BACKGROUND

PHOTOGRAPH DESCRIPTION

SUBJECTS

DATE TAKEN

LOCATION

HISTORY / BACKGROUND

PHOTOGRAPH DESCRIPTION

SUBJECTS

DATE TAKEN

LOCATION

HISTORY / BACKGROUND

Photograph Details

PHOTOGRAPH DESCRIPTION

SUBJECTS

DATE TAKEN

LOCATION

HISTORY / BACKGROUND

PHOTOGRAPH DESCRIPTION

SUBJECTS

DATE TAKEN

LOCATION

HISTORY / BACKGROUND

PHOTOGRAPH DESCRIPTION

SUBJECTS

DATE TAKEN

LOCATION

HISTORY / BACKGROUND

Photograph Details

PHOTOGRAPH DESCRIPTION

SUBJECTS

DATE TAKEN

LOCATION

HISTORY / BACKGROUND

PHOTOGRAPH DESCRIPTION

SUBJECTS

DATE TAKEN

LOCATION

HISTORY / BACKGROUND

PHOTOGRAPH DESCRIPTION

SUBJECTS

DATE TAKEN

LOCATION

HISTORY / BACKGROUND

Photograph Details

PHOTOGRAPH DESCRIPTION

SUBJECTS

DATE TAKEN

LOCATION

HISTORY / BACKGROUND

PHOTOGRAPH DESCRIPTION

SUBJECTS

DATE TAKEN

LOCATION

HISTORY / BACKGROUND

PHOTOGRAPH DESCRIPTION

SUBJECTS

DATE TAKEN

LOCATION

HISTORY / BACKGROUND

Photograph Details

PHOTOGRAPH DESCRIPTION

SUBJECTS

DATE TAKEN

LOCATION

HISTORY / BACKGROUND

PHOTOGRAPH DESCRIPTION

SUBJECTS

DATE TAKEN

LOCATION

HISTORY / BACKGROUND

PHOTOGRAPH DESCRIPTION

SUBJECTS

DATE TAKEN

LOCATION

HISTORY / BACKGROUND

Photograph Details

PHOTOGRAPH DESCRIPTION

SUBJECTS

DATE TAKEN

LOCATION

HISTORY / BACKGROUND

PHOTOGRAPH DESCRIPTION

SUBJECTS

DATE TAKEN

LOCATION

HISTORY / BACKGROUND

PHOTOGRAPH DESCRIPTION

SUBJECTS

DATE TAKEN

LOCATION

HISTORY / BACKGROUND

End of Life Instructions

FUNERAL HOME		
CONTACT		
PHONE		
EMAIL		
STREET ADDRESS		
CITY	STATE	ZIP

BURIAL PLOT #		
CONTACT		
PHONE		
LOCATION		
STREET ADDRESS		
CITY	STATE	ZIP

SERVICE DETAILS		
LOCATION		
STREET ADDRESS		
CITY	STATE	ZIP
TIME OF DAY		
OFFICIANT		
PALL BEARERS		
EULOGY		
READERS		
MUSIC		
FLOWERS		

Oh, And About Those Bodies...

Scan here for more useful books, journals, and notebooks

Find a Journal For Any Occasion

Lined Journals
Travel Journals
Book Club Journals
Bible Study Journals
Sewing Journals
Meal Planning Journals

MORE JOURNALS AND BOOKS AVAILABLE AT
Amazon.com/Author/BackyardBirdNerd

Cover and page design by Cheryl Johnson

BirdNerdPublishing.com
©Bird Nerd Publishing

Made in the USA
Las Vegas, NV
09 July 2024

92029967R00069